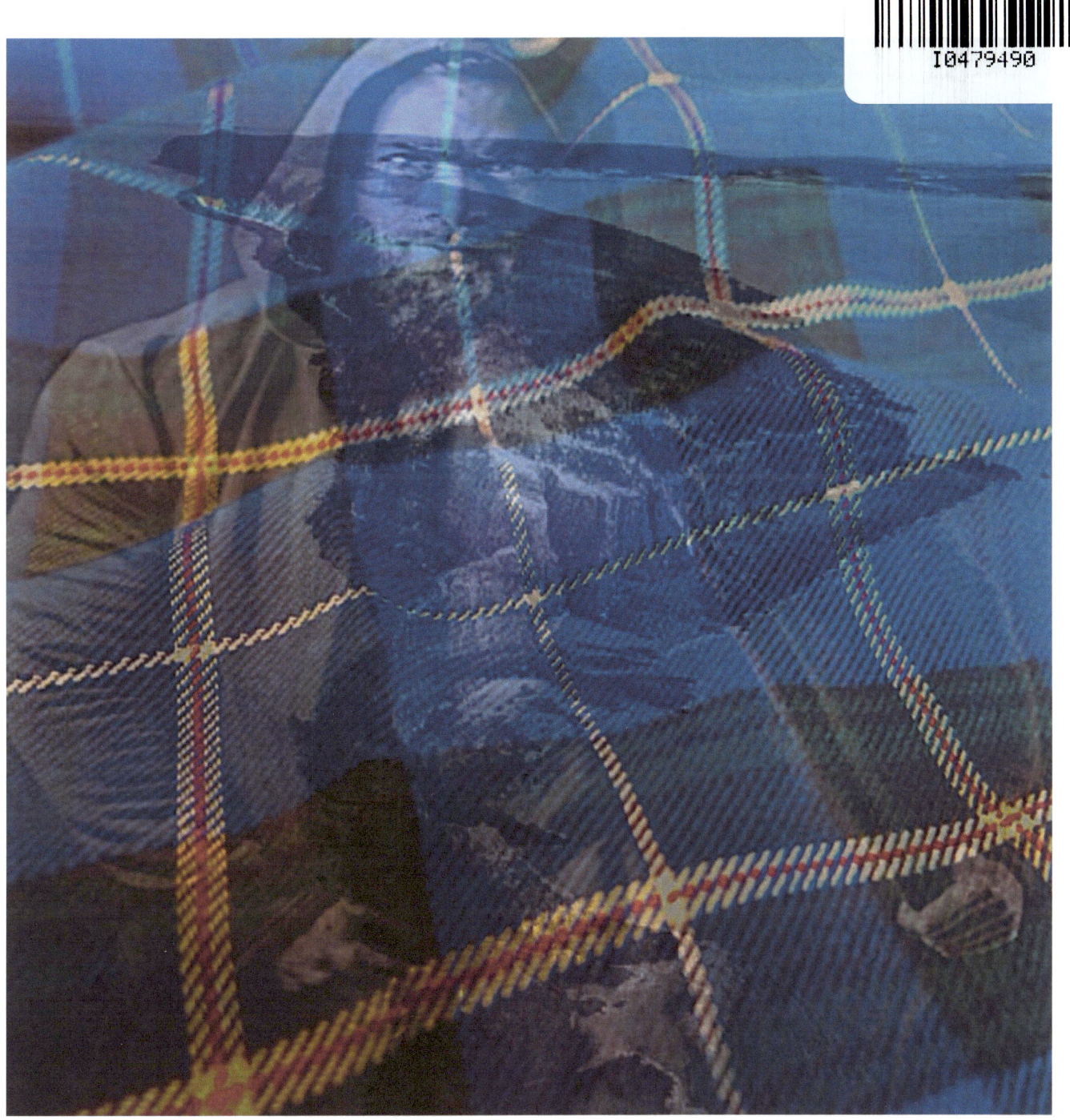

This Book is dedicated to the following:

The marginalized Visual artists Shining a light
of Therapeutic empathy onto
Terres des Hommes world. In a time where
we are witnessing the very collapse of meaning itself.
Hence, the urgency to shine a brave and fearless light
onto the <u>Wetiko-fueled darkness of racism</u> and banish
it from our French Acadian Culture for good.

Mississippi Acadia Goddam

Chapter 1: Introduction to Acadie's Oligarchal Hunger Games Template Ineptocracy Culture

Straight out of a Tourist brochure is Acadie, a region steeped in French Acadian traditions, with its unique and antiquated oligarchal system that runs the Heritage Patrimonial industry like a gang of Cultural Ambassadors. The poor ghetto population of Claregyle follows it like a herd of lambs year after year since that is the way it has always been.

From Pride and Prejudice-infested Oligarchs who run the Heritage, Patrimonial Industry, this book manifesto explores this system's historical and cultural roots and its negative impact on stifling creativity and innovation, hence the death of Acadian culture due to creative bankruptcy.

It is all done or undone by centuries-old traditions of political connections, from rumours on the dirty old senator to 52 cases of aggravated sexual assault on the campus of Université Ste Anne under a rug swept in a don`t ask, don't tell culture. Yet big as you please, Queer Aspergers Contemporary Artist Theriault continues with multiple media platform callouts to uncover and eliminate the hidden barriers of entry that are stifling innovation and keeping him ghosted for half a century.

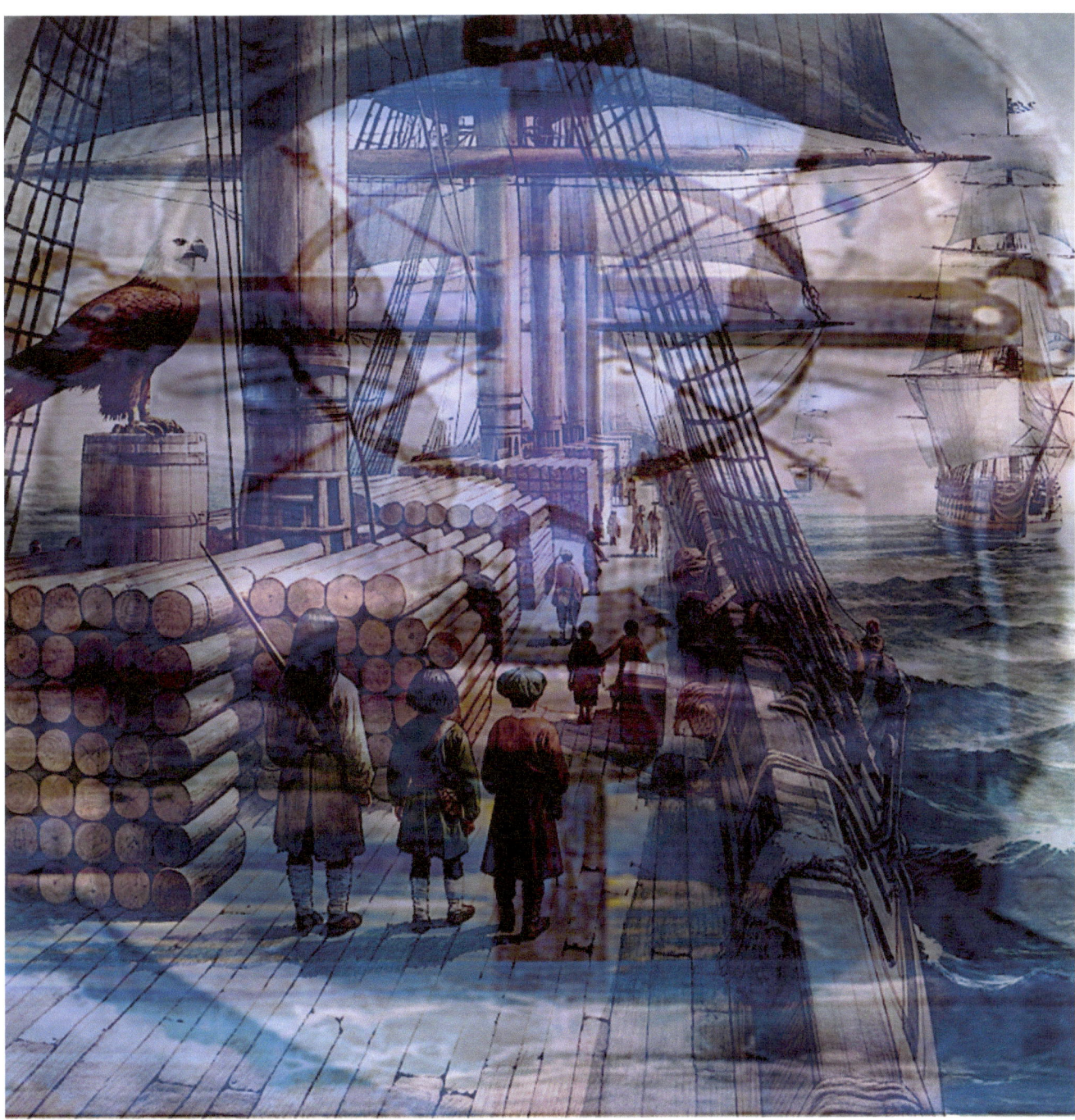

Chapter 2: The Oligarchal Power Structure as Saturn Devours His Children Opera Style

Please do your due diligence research to Delve deeper into the mechanisms of <u>Acadie's oligarchy power structure</u>, focusing on examining how it consolidates control and suppresses dissent who do not follow the Straight White Roman Catholic herd mentality.

Look for the highlighted real-life examples and anecdotes illustrating It influenced how the Phil Comeau film The Secret Order of Jacques Cartier spoke of the oppressors being English for decades. It turned it around to show how the new self-serving, politically connected Oligarch Clan Bovine is the new enemy.

Le Nouveau's enemy du jour is now within the Acadian culture. And Theriault is OK with that. We all have agreed to disagree and finalize efforts to engage in discourse. Your role is crucial in this. The past 50-year chapter ends with realizing the pervasive nature of oligarchal control in Acadie until they die: Ainsi Soi T'il Yo' Honey.

Peuple Acajun Peuple Acajun ou tu tèn vas avec le Jatre en Charre Vieux Jatre en Charre rien autre que le vieux Jatre en Charre Peuple Acajun Dis Dis Dis Nous la Woire...

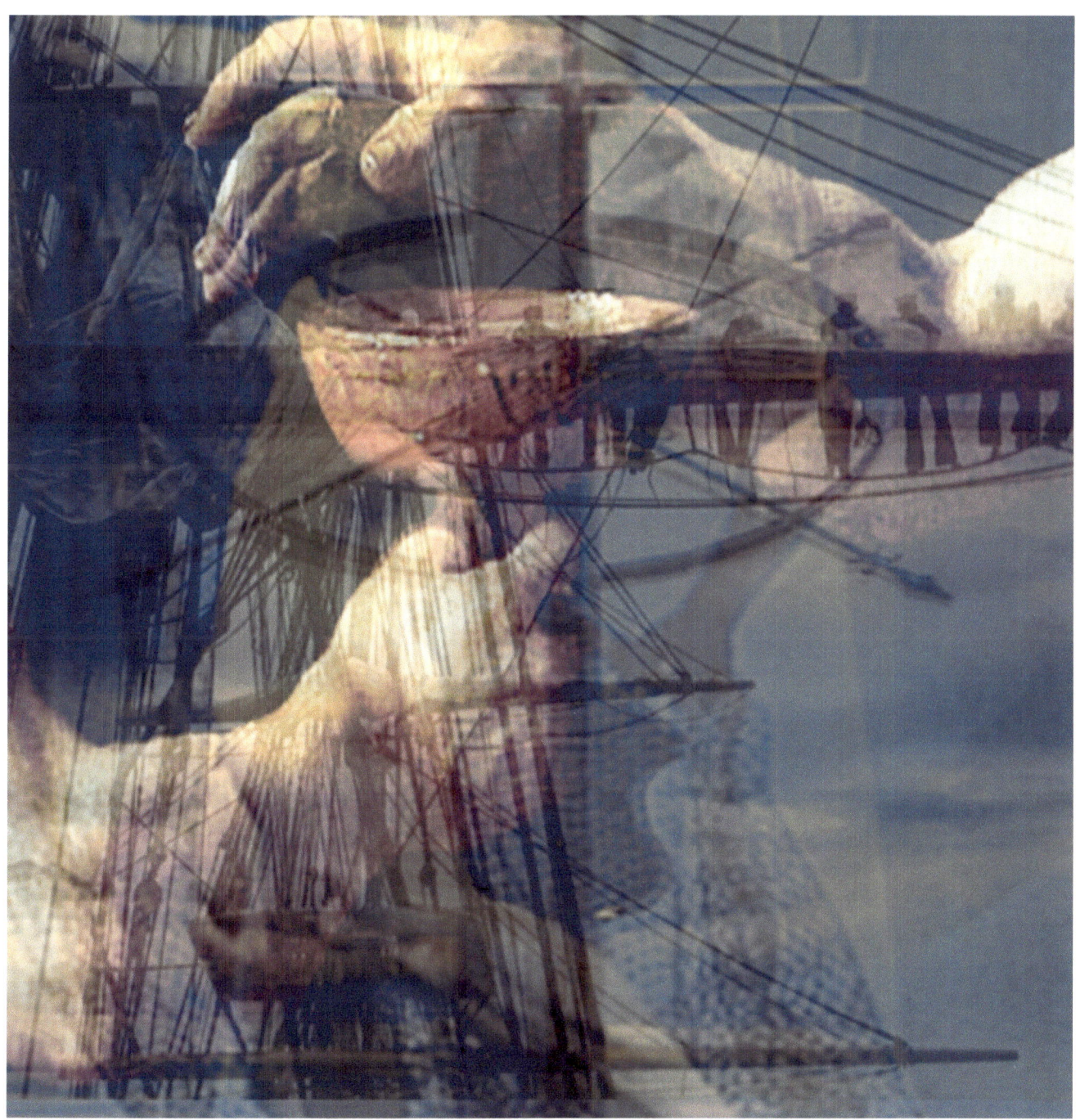

Chapter 3: Balancing Tradition and Innovation in Acadian Culture

In Acadian communities, tension exists between preserving cultural heritage and embracing creative evolution. This tension is palpable among those who recognize a tipping point where tradition meets innovation. Traditionally, Acadian cultural events have centred around Country Bluegrass music, perpetuating jigs and reels year after year.

Endeavours supported by government funding.
The entrenched bureaucracy further stifles progress, with cultural diplomats operating with impunity, indifferent to outside voices. Attempts to engage with these bodies often result in Ghosting non-reply silence, reinforcing the perception of a system rigged against change. Ultimately, Acadian culture is at a crossroads, facing multiple missed opportunities for growth due to a reluctance to adapt to changing times.

The failure to fully integrate with mainstream media exacerbates this issue, isolating Acadian voices from our society's broader discourse. The need for cultural adaptation and integration is not just a matter of survival but a crucial step towards ensuring Acadian culture's continued relevance and vibrancy. Instead of simply allowing it to slip into the cultural assimilation that the Kjipuktuk Bastille would love to see go. Bell media does nothing to mention the culture except on August 15th.

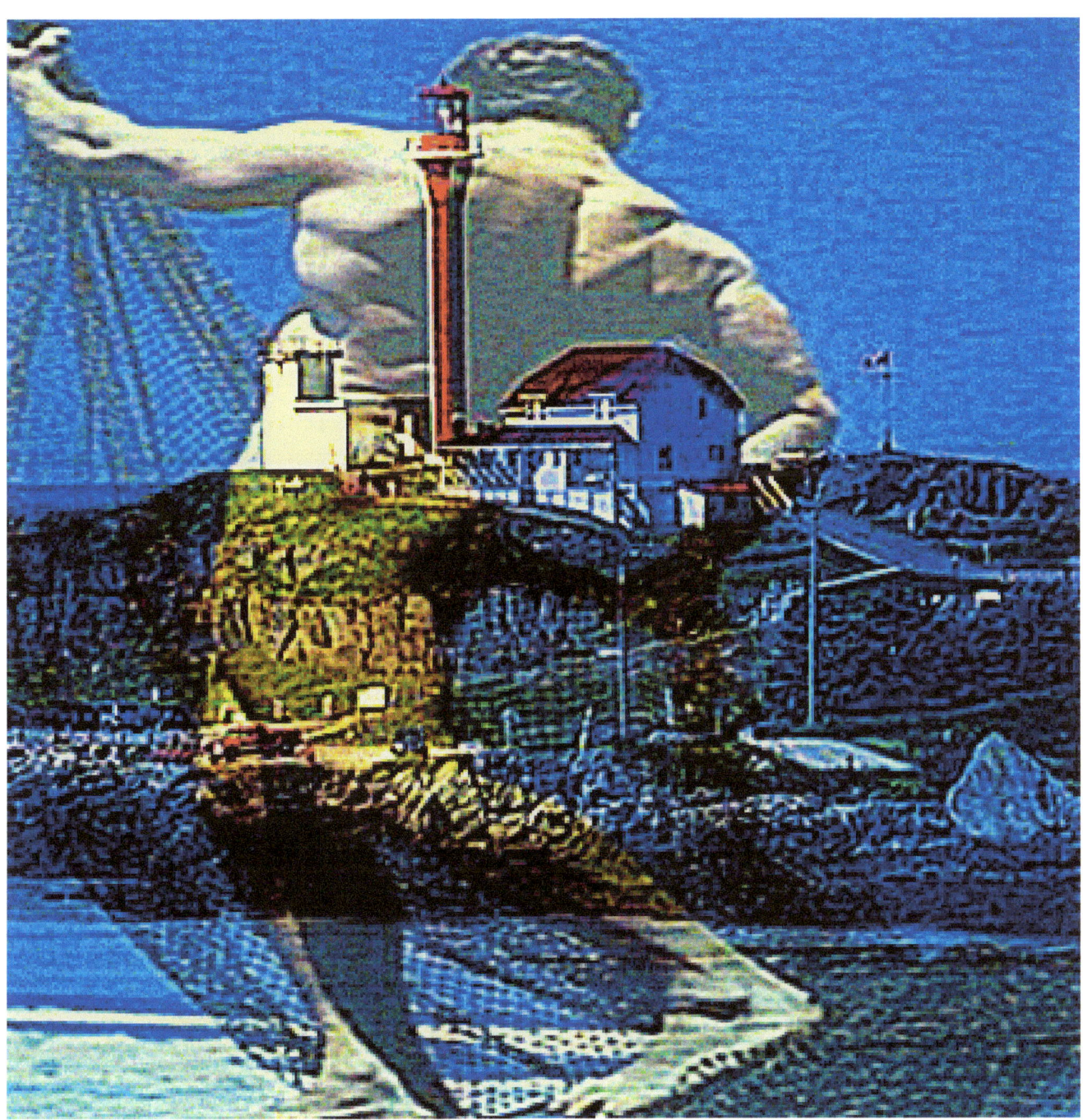

Chapter 4: Dichotomy in Quebecois Progressivism Acadian Conservatism

Meanwhile, in Liberal, forward-thinking and uninhibited Québec, we have world-class arts and culture. Mise en scene by Robert Lepage, Acadians has Le theatre de la Saqouine, Cinematic moments like Dennis Arcand having Rufus Wainwright singing a sacred aria from on high as the opening scene in L'âge des ténèbres.

While we have Trécarré. Quebec has Leonard Cohen's lyrics, and Acadians have ptit Belliveau. Hence, our proud and noble Acadie has the welfare trash label. The Ballad of B Comeau drove Michelin's evergreen factory away to Bridgewater in 1970.

Could someone review the curriculum and teaching methods that reinforce this pattern to recognize the need for educational reform to nurture creativity? It is not different from what I see in youth culture in French schools, where people cannot say two sentences in French without defaulting to English all the time.

There is also a big factor that is big enough for a book on how French Canadian culture in Quebec is liberal and progressive. In contrast, french acadian culture in atlantic canada is conservative and backward thinking, which is key in moving Quebec culture forward in its creativity. In comparison, to acadian culture which remains frozen in time year after year.

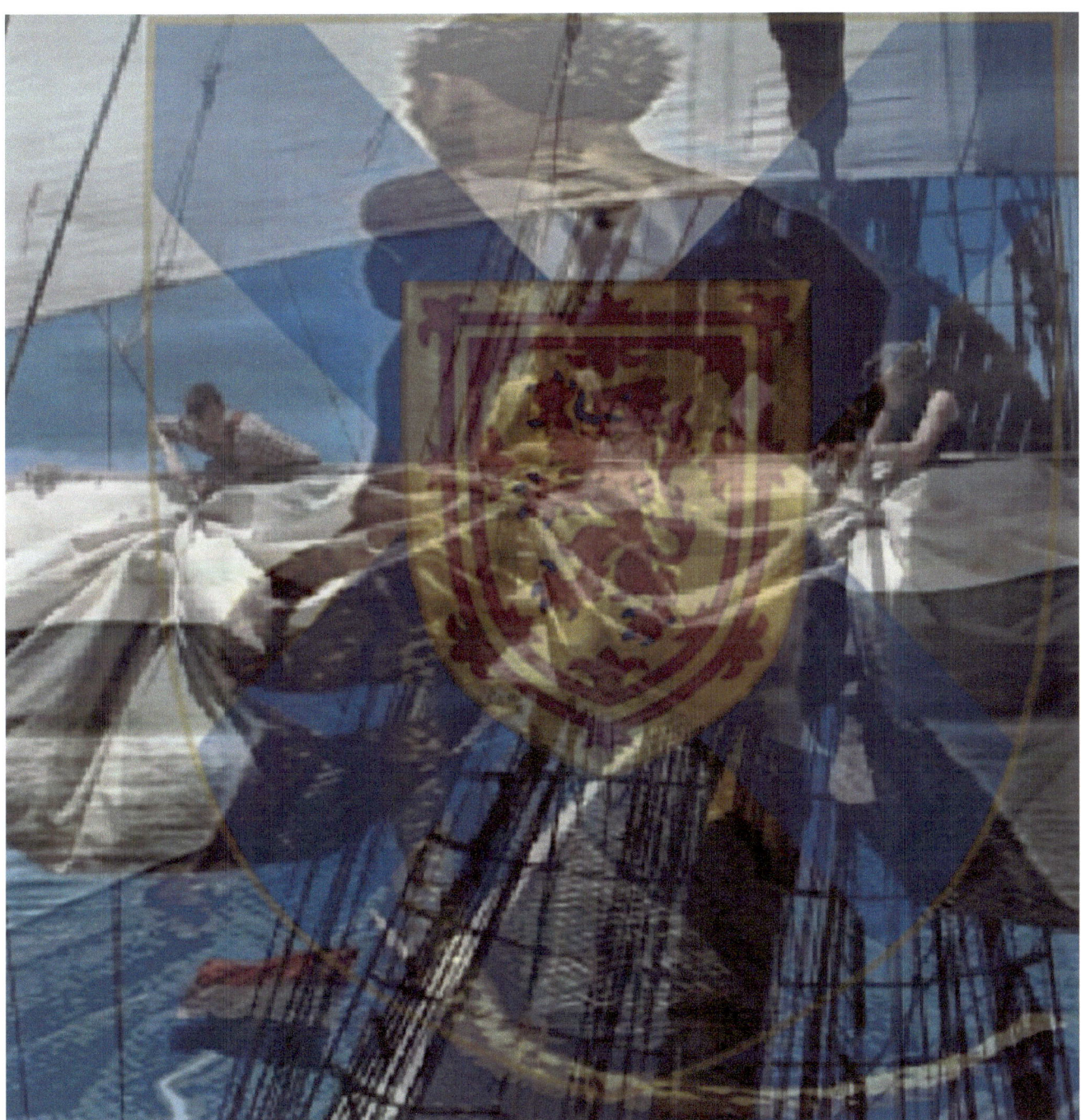

Chapter 5: Economic Stagnation and Risk Aversion in the Cultural Goulag Ghetto Feedback Loop is the same as ever.

For example, the economic landscape of Acadie, Claregyle is characterized by stagnation in its social economics and sociocultural Atlantic Canada ghetto. With La Gang of ego-centric bureaucrat egos stuck in the cultural ambassador and six-figure salary feedback loop year after year, it halts all innovation.

They live in a bubble, and Theriault is OK with that. He lives in a bubble, too, yet he gets up in the morning and goes out to do the challenge of writing the book on the daily challenge of breaking free from the cycle of complacency. He does it as a contemporary artist no one knows of since there is no connection, just ghosting and turning up noses of disdain of the most interesting Queer Aspergers artist voice in Atlantic Canada. Hence, the reason for this book is that a word after a word since a word equals power.

To truly move forward, a culture has to stop continually looking back on its old and tired self. Let the light of creativity shine instead of ghosting it until it goes away, as it will not be going away anytime soon.

So that you know where we are coming from, CMA 2024

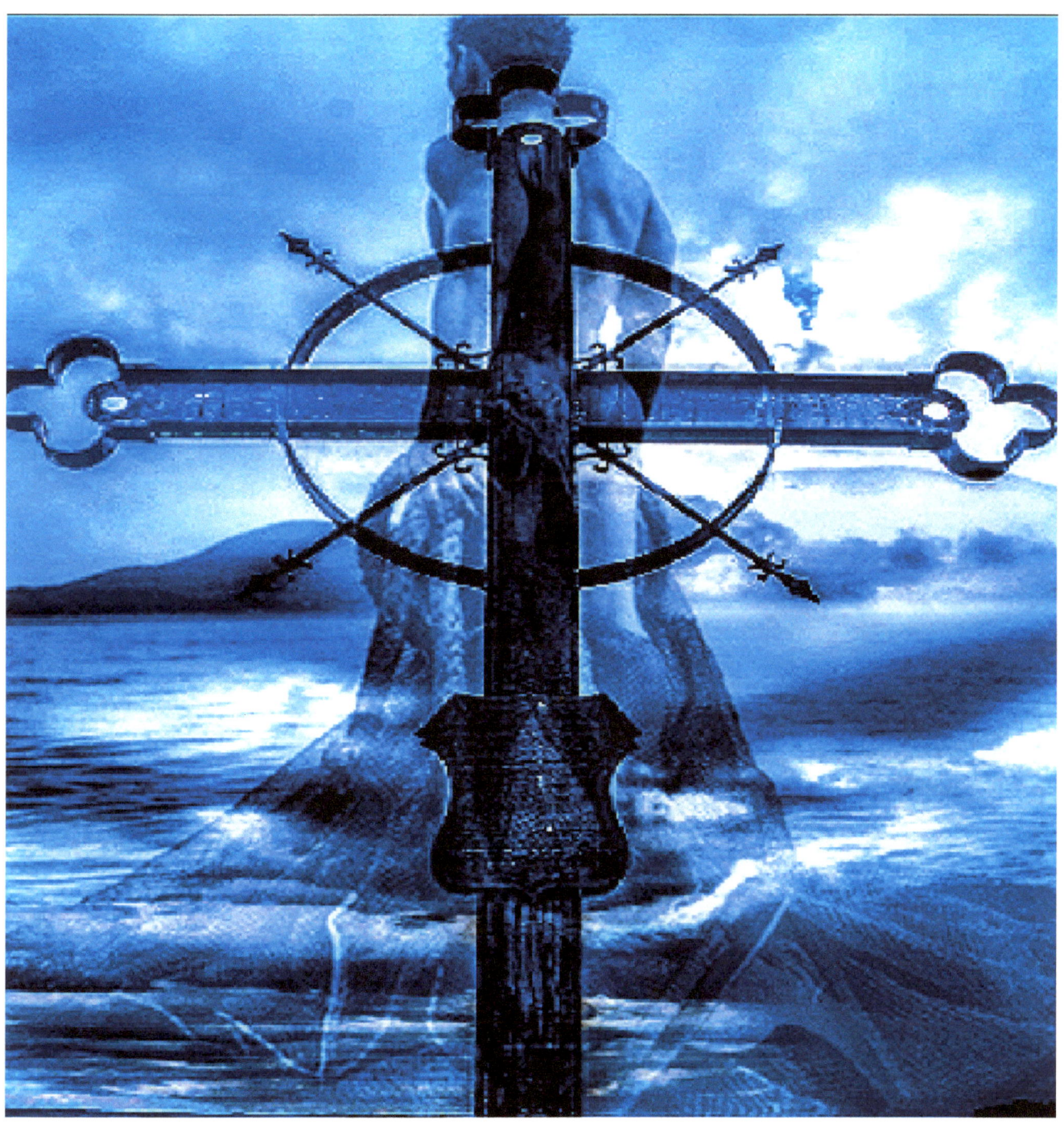

Chapter 6: Freedoms is just another word for nothing left to lose.

In the pre-2030 reset period, the marginalized have nothing to lose. They were calling out Heritage Patrimonial Cultural Institutions as Gatekeepers with their useless there for the paycheck and big pensions to sit on at the end of the line ideologies and Zombie corporations.
More and more locals in the know are seeing the light and expressing how sick and tired we are of walled gardens. The Q in the Local LGBTQ continues to ask for reasons as to why you can ghost, ignore and give out do you know who I am attitude to quote un quote has been musician at the NSLC store in July 2022.
Pure unmitigated gall dished out to a serious Triple Dipped Triple Glaze Queer Asperger Full Spectrum Multi-disciplined Artist type personality like Theriault. Who is currently channelling himself some Jackie and Yvonne Vautour spunk to stand up and demand inclusion instead of racist exclusion?

It runs like clockwork on a template rotten to the core.
Hence, something needs to be done about getting Visual artists included on the Nos Artistes de la Baie list. Visual artists get 2000 square feet, no love, and no money, while musicians get 200,000 square feet, all the love and all the money.

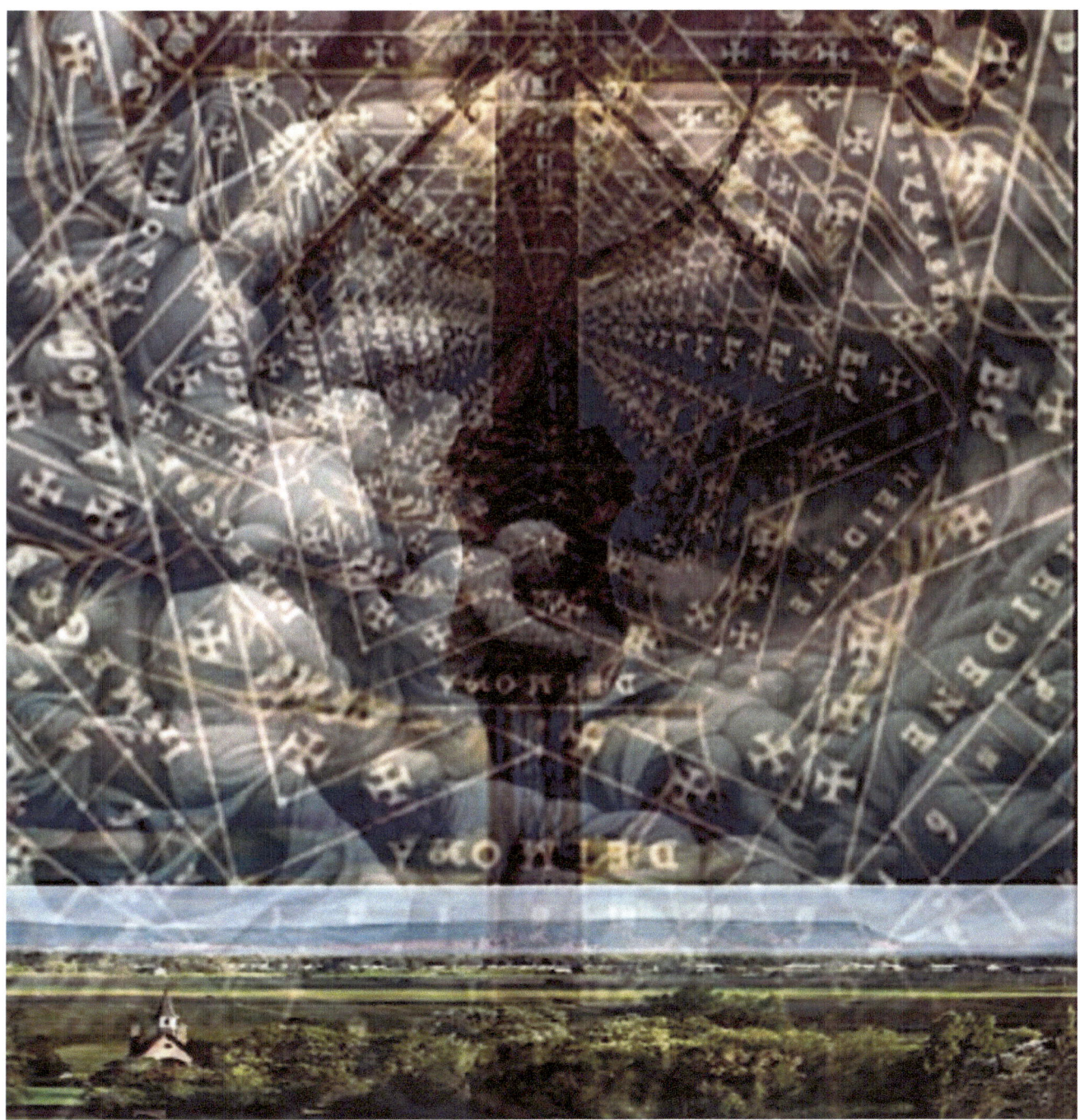

Chapter 7: Like drawing Blood from Stone.

Folks need to examine how cultural institutions act as gatekeepers, preserving the status quo and excluding dissenting voices who happen to have multiple indented listings on the first page of Google due to the merits of their visual artist narratives. Discuss the impact on artistic expression, intellectual discourse, the new NFT blockchain, and AI technological advancement. Claude Edwin Theriault is world-class.

The don`t ask, don`t tell spoken Verboten deal breaker thing with Theriault is that he uses the archetypal Male nude to express Terre des Hommes, meaning the human race. Just like the female nude is used to express the Mother Earth goddess Gaia or Venus as western civilizations call her; artists have used these archetypes for Millannia, yet the prudish Roman catholic powers that be see it all as Verboten meaning forbidden. Claude challenges them on their prudish judgment calls regarding what can be on the cultural ambassador list and what cannot.

While there for the paycheck oligarch Zombie corporations like Productions de la Roche Blue and a French acadian music record label all in English rule. We shall officially end this chapter with a resolve to challenge the hegemony of these institutions and show them some spunk and spirit. With the continuing IG Reels Cajun Dead et Le Talkin' Stick Song lyric project extraordinaire.

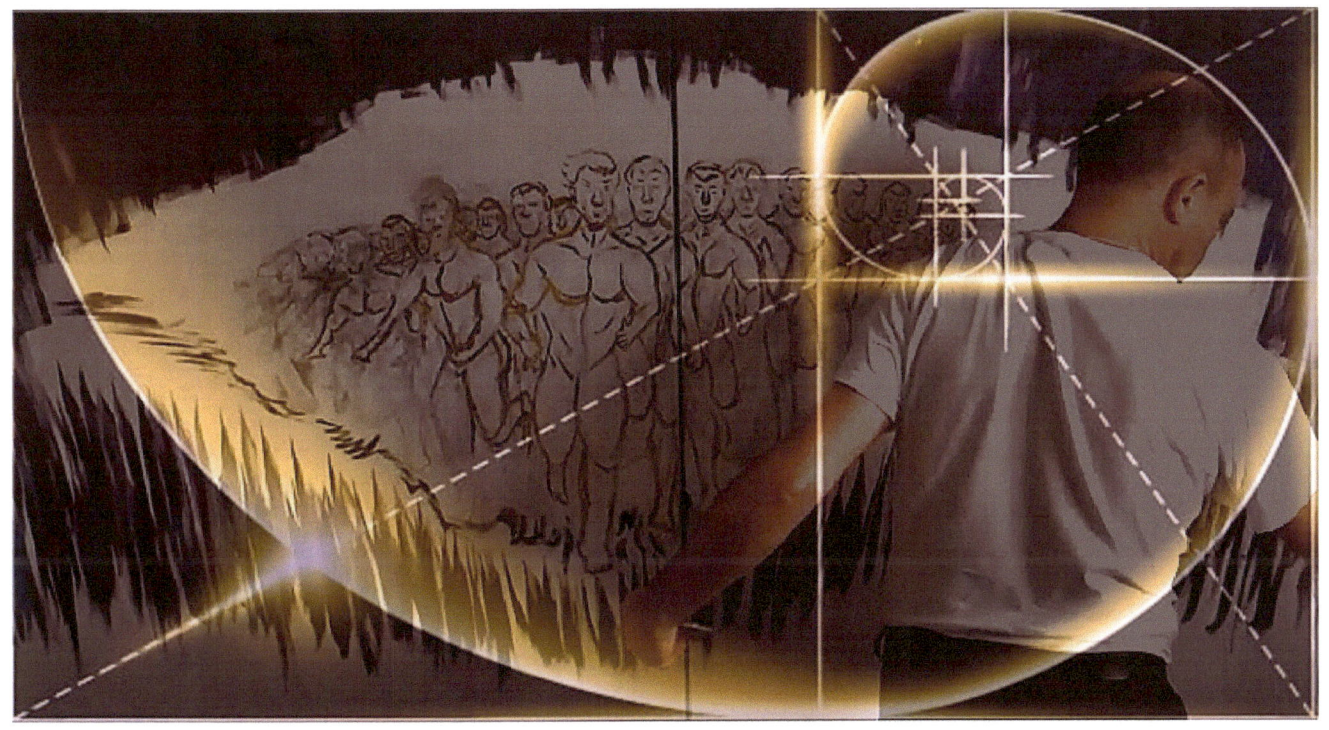

The Heritage Patrimonial Oligarch culture languishes in exhaustion, overwhelmed by a relentless pursuit of wealth and status. These days, there are three kinds of people, "the ones of ability" who know that they can't consume more than they have produced, the ordinary working stiff who attempts to do the best they can with their limited potential, and the ten member Oligarch looters who derive their worth by leeching due to their political connections. Hence, the reason is to call them out when you have nothing to lose; you have everything to gain.

Chapter 8: Resistance and Resilience of just keeping on till you die.

Claude Edwin Theriault has been an active visual artist, creating artworks of great merit since 1974. The Oligarch clic has systematically ghosted him for half a century; hence, his nothing-to-lose callout in the face of the group resistance. Using daily content creation to inspire tenacity
and resilience, found outside Acadie's creative community, asleep at the dull and uninspired wheel.

His 50 years of work showcases his Queer Asperger's individuality and his artworks and NfTs that defy the oligarchal norms. Explore the challenges they face and the SERP content creation strategies he employs to navigate the adversity of the Oligarch who does nothing since they do not have to build a career. However, it has been like that in the art and politics industry since the dawn.

Theriault takes it all with a grain of salt and massive breathwork, with a sense of hope and determination for the change the merit of Theriault's work brings to a creatively bankrupt culture.
You can only do the same old Hill Bill Music and Rappie Pie for so long before a culture goes creatively bankrupt due to a lack of innovation.

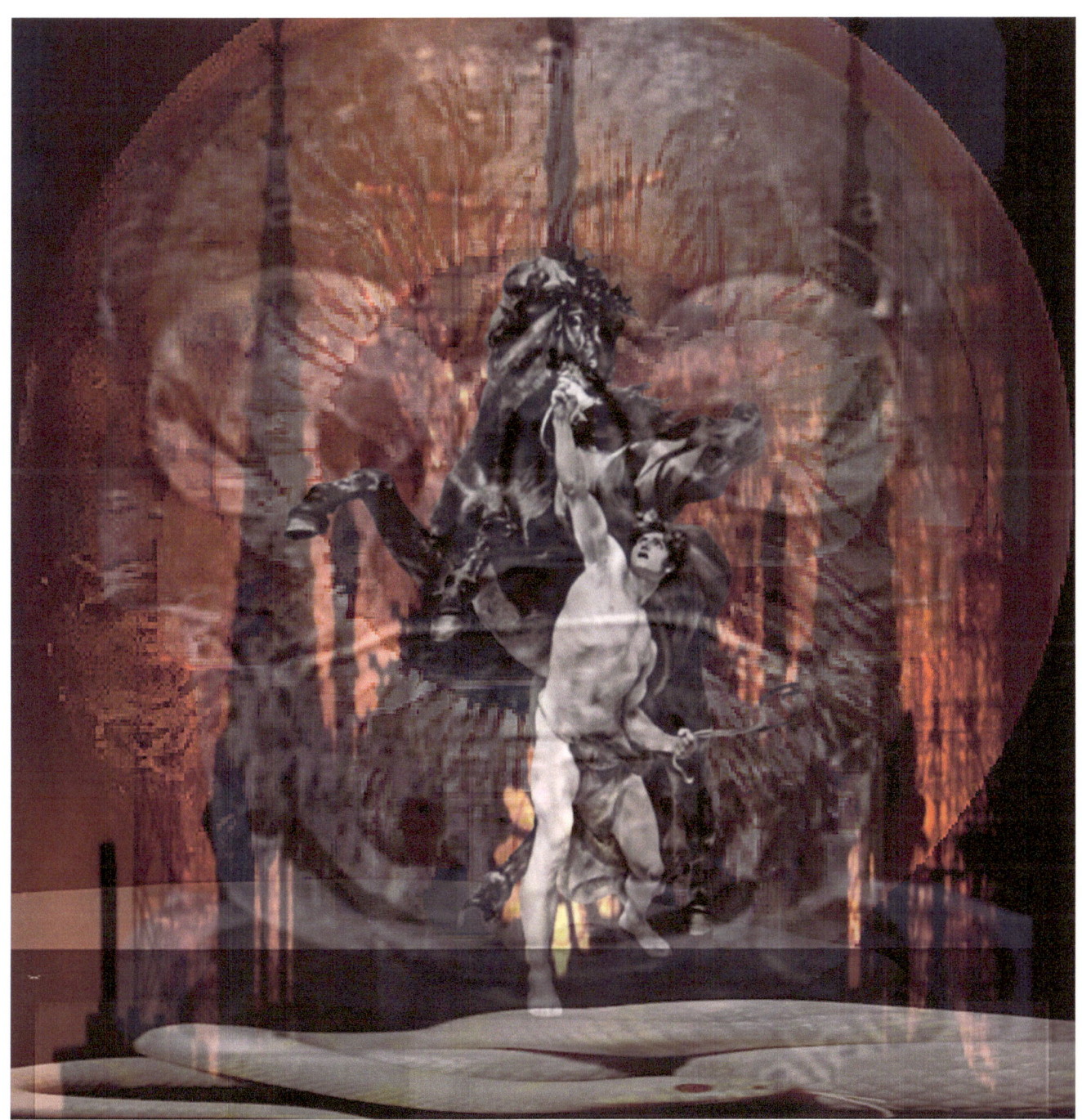

Chapter 9: Bridging Web2 Traditions and Web3 Innovation

Theriault does not Propose strategies. He builds and deploys them from Communique de Presse to NFT to a newsletter or two for bridging Acadian traditions with innovative practices, emphasizing synergy rather than conflict- solution rather than a cause. Theriault proposes embracing the enemy. He has a POD and NFT Collection of La Bastille de Charles Menoux D'Aulnay lui-meme in the Tour de Charles de Menou Dàulney, and folks laugh at him as <u>he continues to disrupt the frustrating feedback loop</u> of the same old.

It's no problem; all is crashing and burning anyway on the way to the great Rest 2030; we will all need a busload of Fath to get by and start living the initiatives that embrace heritage and creativity, fostering a dynamic cultural landscape.

Let us close this chapter with a resolute vision for a more inclusive and vibrant Acadie. It's time for change, for a shift away from stagnant and uninspired entities like Zombie corporations. Zombie corporations like, a French-language record label all in English, with their dull and uninspired POD and the latest greatest album nobody buys. And let's not forget the Merch POD by East Coast Lifestyle, the official merch supplier of CMA 2024, a testament to our dynamic and evolving culture. The biggest Halifax-centric and francophobic gang in town...go figure.

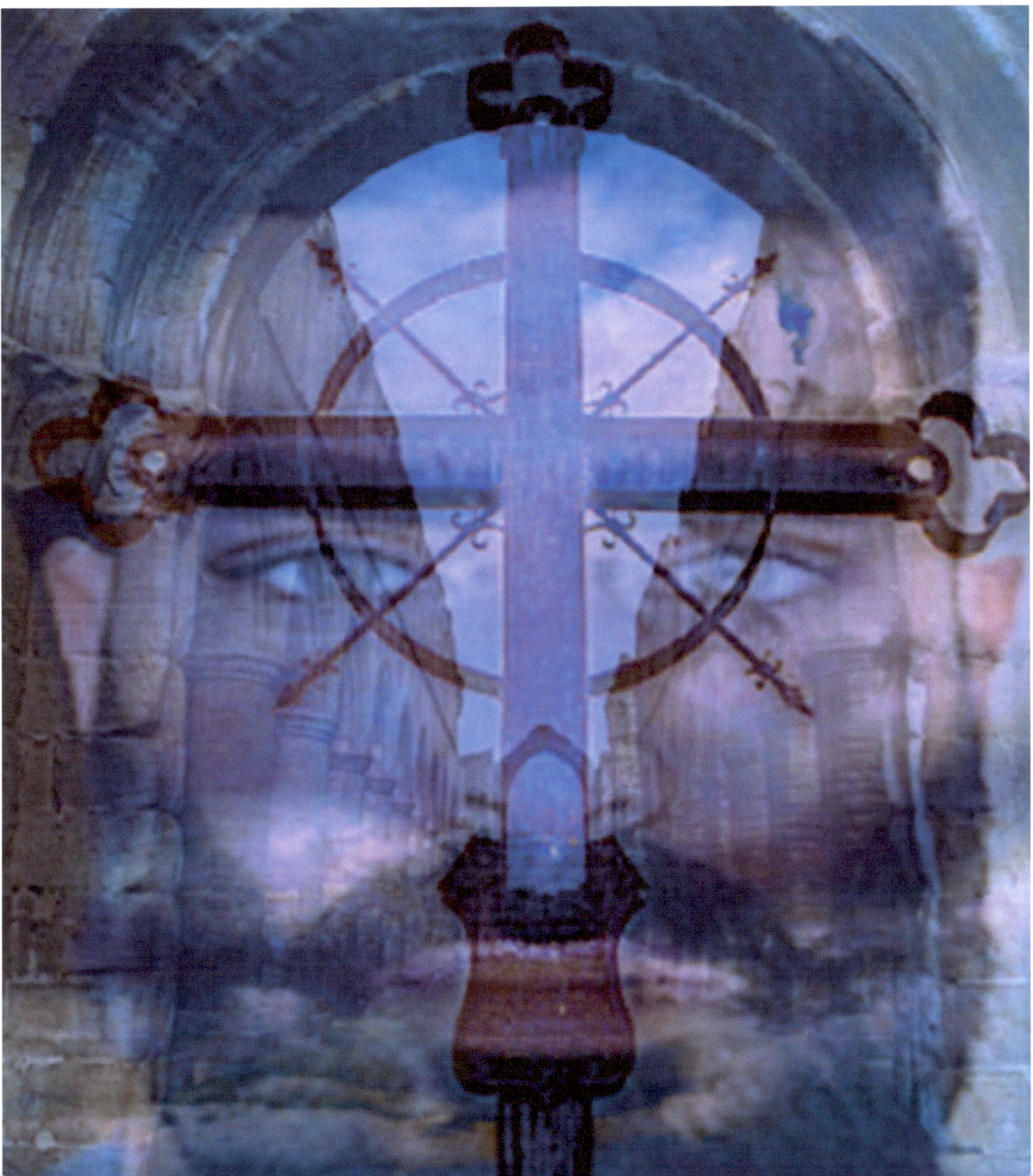

Chapter 10: Shamanic Shape-Shifting Seeds of Change, whether you like it or not, Honey.

Theriault continues to Investigate emerging NFT and AI trends and movements, using the censor-free publishing mediums of Blockchain.io nodes sites; to call out and challenge the oligarchal grip on Acadie, from grassroots activism to the Q in local LGBTQ Claregyle cultural renaissance in the visual arts, that have to say in La liste de nos artistes de la Baie Sainte Honkie Marie.

Theriault and his MBF-Lifestyle design studio, as well as the Cajun Dead and Le Walkin`Stick publishing, Cajun Dead and Le Talkin`Stick exploring actual song lyrics that make sense and express a heartfelt sentiment that has allure. Instead of singing, I got my cheque from the tax return going to go to the liquor store, going to get me a bunch of 649s cause I got my cheque from the tax return... and call it the cat's ass instead of the ghetto welfare drug and alcoholism currently endemic in Claregyle.

At this point in the cycle, there has been so much abuse of the system and a growing loss of public trust that politicians know it can't be saved. So why not just drive it all into the ground?

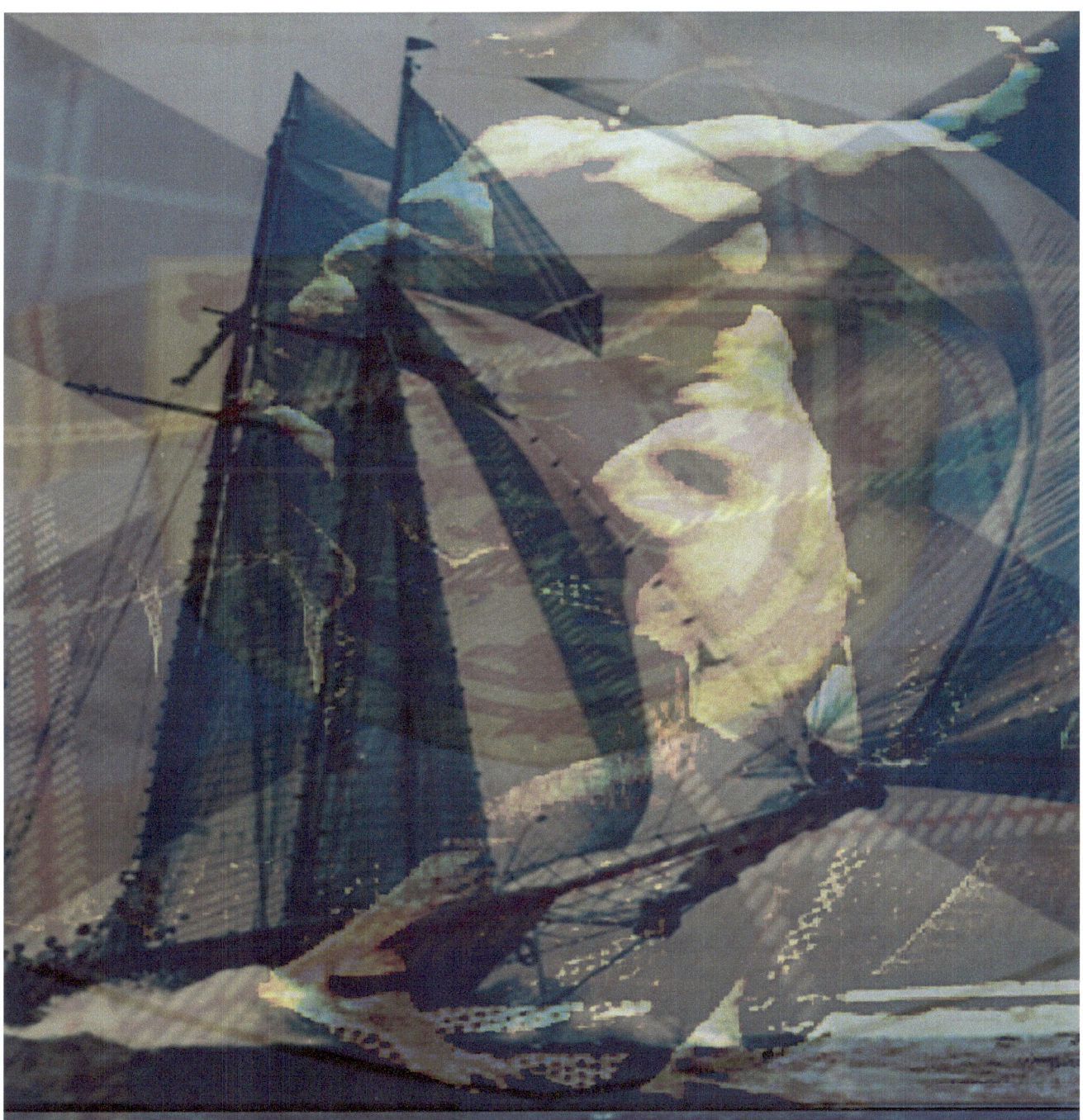

Chapter 11: Transformation by Fire.

Theriault explores the potential catalysts for transformative change and the barriers he faces since the culture is at an arts and crafts level. At the same time, Theriault is a multi-media inspired by Totemic <u>Archetypal 3D Motion Graphic NFTs.</u>
They were inspired by Appalachian Cajun Dead et Le Talkin Stick Sung Hung Acapella song lyric, with the latest MBF-Lifestyle Publishing Cajun Dead et Le Walkin`Stick Acadian Diaspora 1755. It is a child refugee parable narrative with illustrations depicting sentinel beings in a dreamscape from a Disney movie. Constant production of projects creative design experts from on high `Yet no media in Nova Scotia or Cajun culture mentions any of this since they are all on the same ghosting by herd design page.

And Theriault is OK with it. He is his platform and, as such, does not participate in any of their wing-ding festive events since it is all a series of glass-walled gardens of Clics to the right who do not speak to the clic on the left who does not talk to the clic in the middle, with none of them speaking to Theriault since they are that Insular; and Theriault moves forward with anticipation for the future and what his efforts are single-handedly bringing to it.

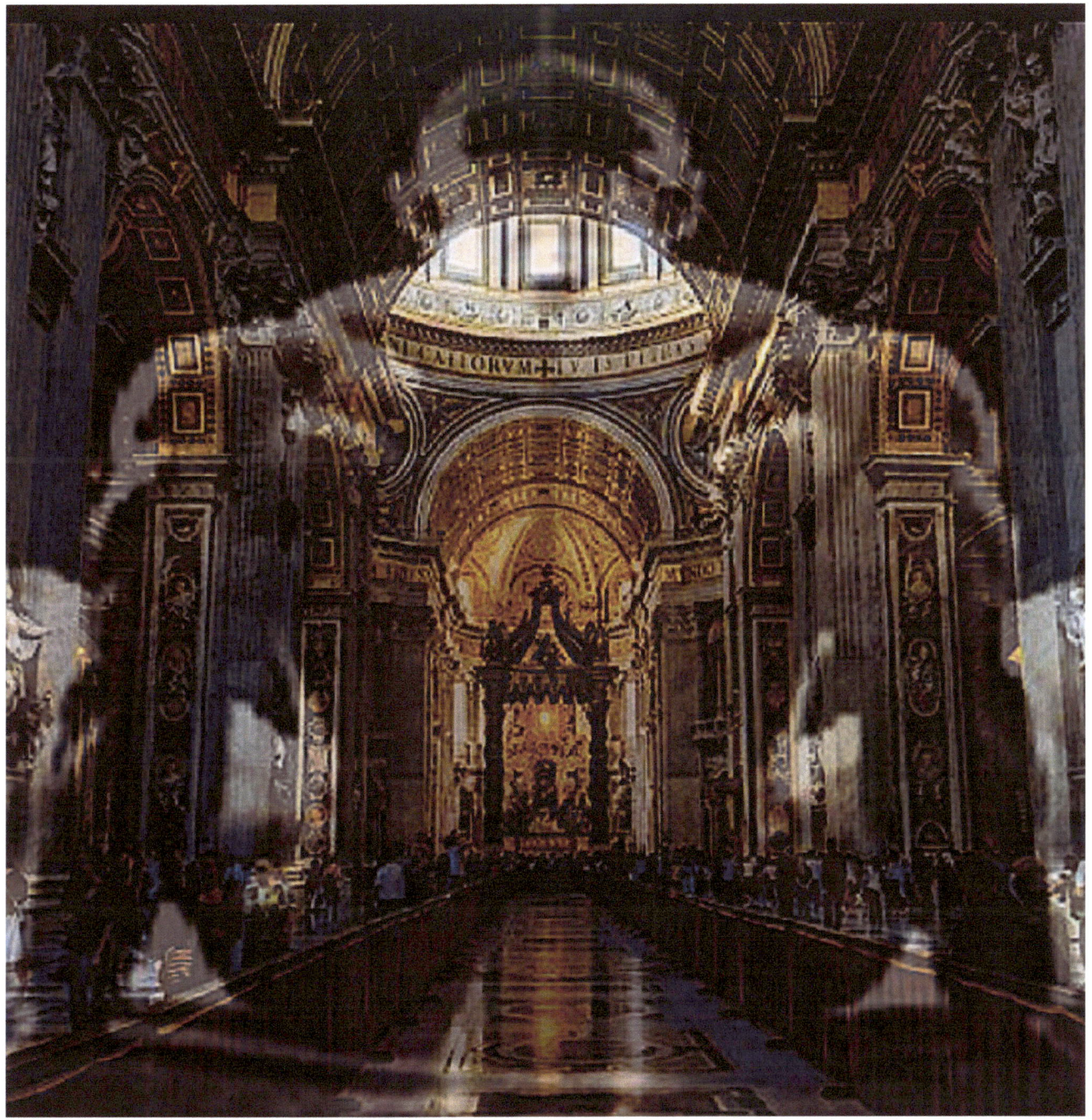

Chapter 12: The number one source of Dharma is attachment; let it go

Moving towards a Creative Renaissance and Je M`en absolve de l'affaire since there is no choice but to move La Culture Cajun forward instead of frozen in the Goulag Ghetto feedback of the past.

Trouble will soon be over, and Sorrow will have an end to conclude with a small but growing number of people who want a future where Acadie embraces full spectrum inclusion, creativity, and innovation for real instead of having East Coast Lifestyle merch like uninspired posters and T-shirts that promote it but do not walk the walk.

Instead of old, antiquated, frozen-in-time archetypes of Evangeline, Gabriel, Grand Pré and the 1755 deportation cookie-cutter templates with oligarchal constraints and nothing else.
Until it all stops working or being funded by the government, the <u>ruling oligarchs need to change their tune and be inclusive for real</u> instead of pretend Inclusion.
They are still at the Grade 10 level of cool kids like us, not cool kids like them, which is not the mindset to have if you want to be a cultural ambassador.

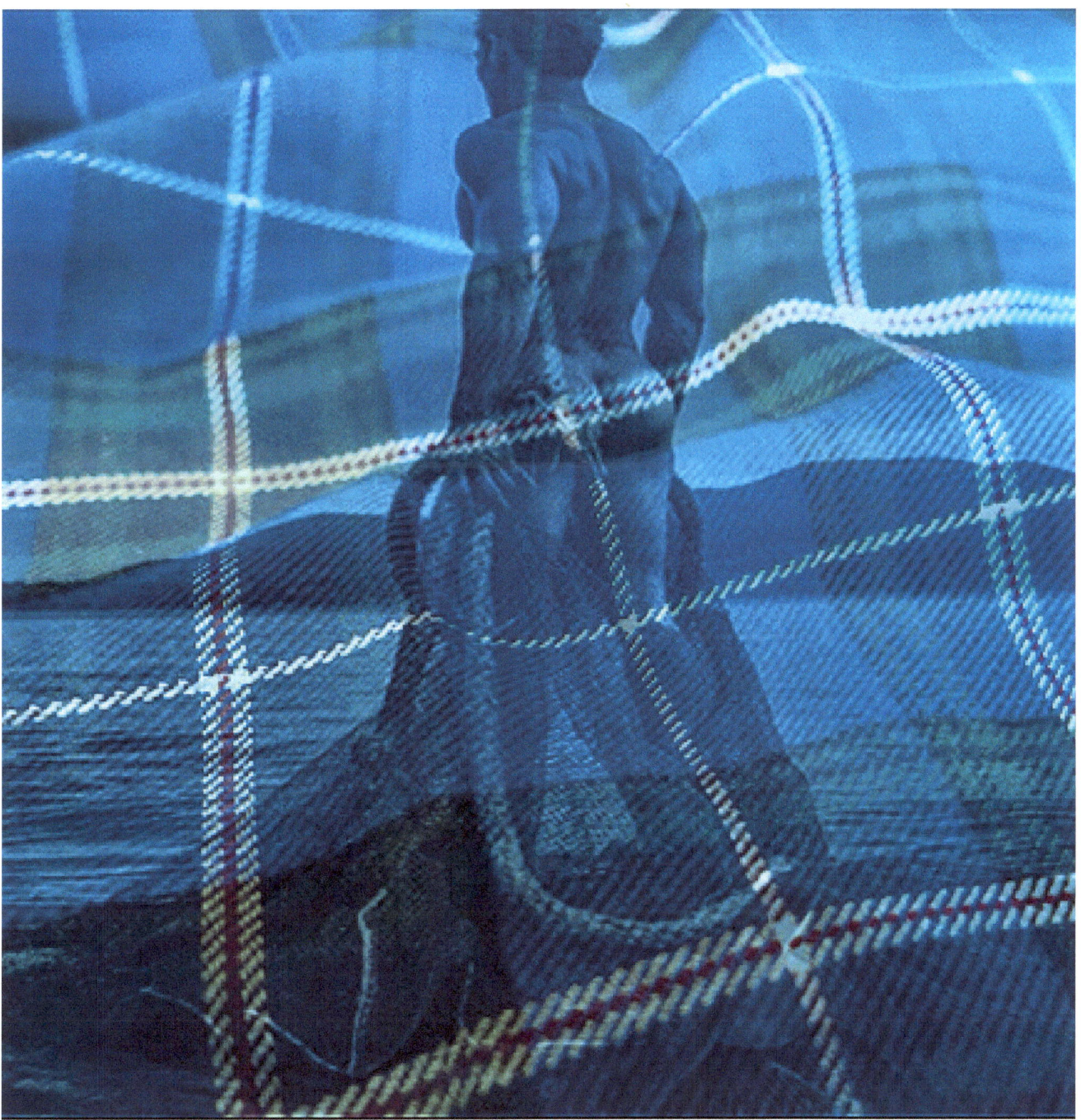

Chapter 13: Zombie Corporations I Have Known

In keeping with zombie corporation Standard Operating Procedures, the artists from the Bay have all been one-hit wonders, who has not done anything since 1990. Yet they
are what the local Patois talk calls Fourré, meaning connected in the non-profit, therefore non-liable, meaning you cannot sue them for being Honky racist; smart cover move in the Heritage Patrimonial chess game they play. Since it is a modern standard play of your basic Opera template, that's OK. However, you can call them out on their hypocrisy since word after word after word equals power, so read on with wild abandon since they say it gets better.... I don't know when, where, or how. But you never know.

After all, here you are reading this book that tells it to you from the Odd&Old Man Out Queer Asperger's, with exclusion being given to Claude Edwin Theriault.
Only by taking a collective set of actionable steps to build a more open and inclusive society that nurtures creative talent will we move a culture that needs moving forward. Since a culture that always looks back on its proud and noble past will never move forward, it will continue to slip into the assimilation that it is sinking into with youths that cannot say two sentences in a row in French since they are immersed in an Anglo.
Tic Tok culture of nothing.

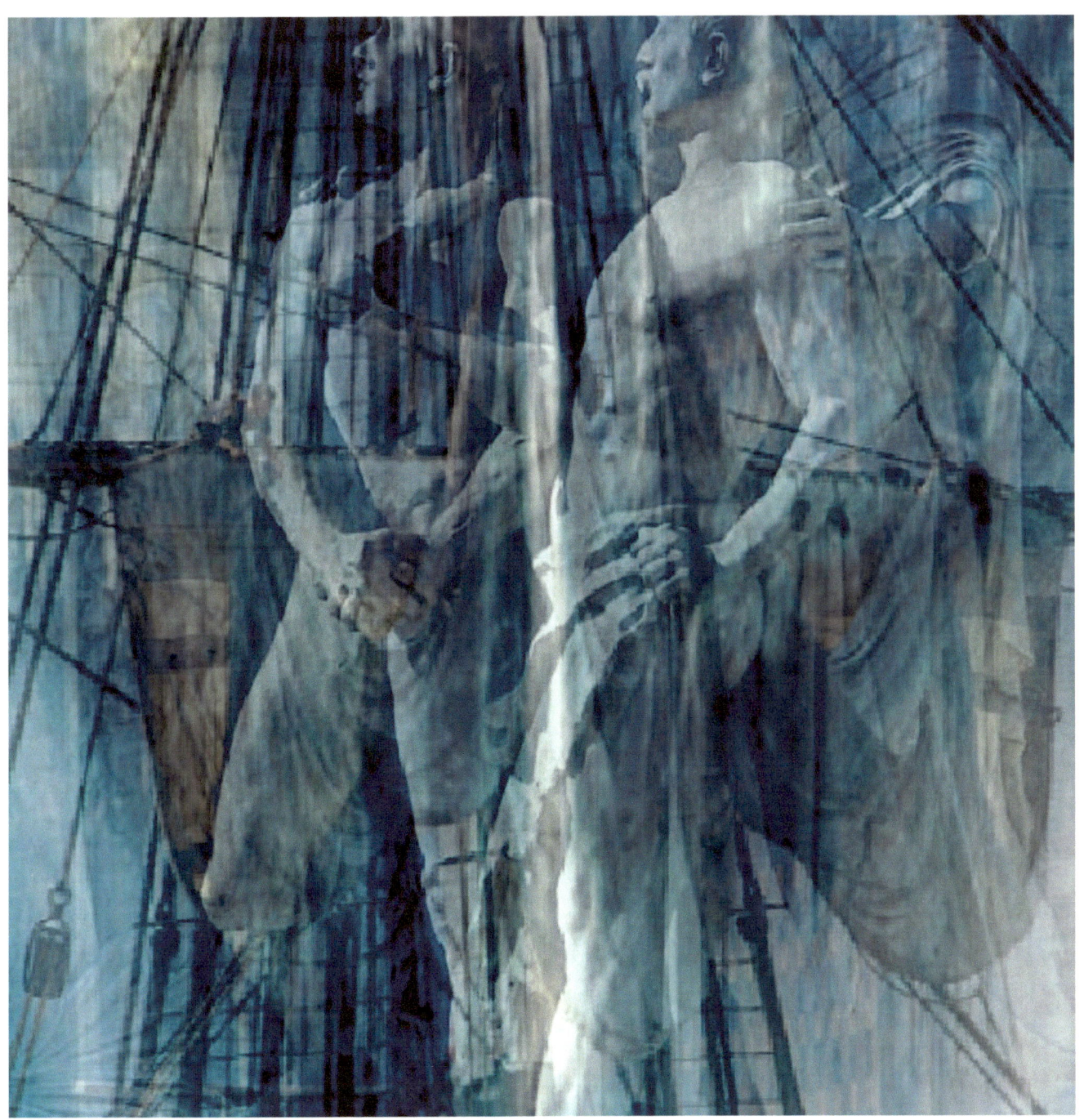

Chapter 14: All with no template are lost

Hence, the youth who do not have an innovative or creative platform of expression are lost.

Having Arrêt on the traffic stop signs in Halifax will not save the culture, endless mindless months on an anal retentive passive aggressive Bill-C This and Bill C That is just paperwork as useful as a pair of tits on a bull.

Giving them a song lyric project that shows the sheer beauty of their language when it is broken down phonetically and typed into the subheadings of a sung acapella song narrative with one of a series of 3D Motion Graphic NFTs to look at while you breathe in deep through the nose and calm ya self; since that is the what comes from the hand of Thaeriault in his creative templates and pallets he creates like a new form of a Fabergé egg with hanging from the gallows pole song narrative you can dig and build an Appalachian songbook with.

Let's move on from the old and tired cash cow agenda of Getting service in a government office in French in a province where Acadians are 10% and functionally incapable of reading or writing French. This wastes time and resources in a provincial and government industry that officially has yet to learn since its template is broken.

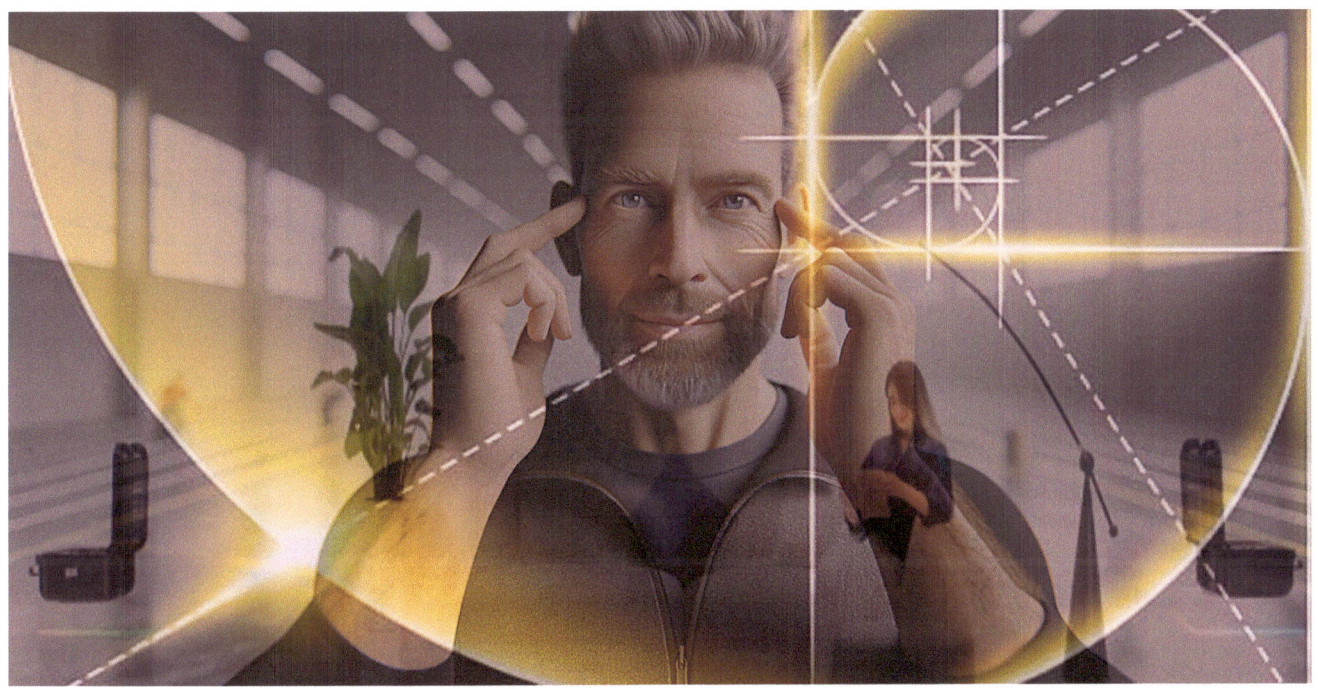

Quebec culture propels forward with dynamic initiatives, embracing modernity while preserving tradition. Meanwhile, Acadian culture faces challenges in maintaining its distinct identity. To shift this trend, collaborative efforts are vital. Investing in Acadian arts, education, and community projects fosters pride and continuity. Encouraging cultural exchanges between Quebec and Acadian regions cultivates mutual appreciation and revitalizes Acadian heritage. They say that embracing diversity within Canada strengthens the nation's cultural fabric. Yet, there is that invisible don`t ask, don`t tell side to Acadian Culture, hence the need to grant full inclusion to the Q in the LGBTQ gang in the gosh darn golly maritime neighbourhood for a change to occur.

Chapter 15: Kijpuktuk calls you to La Bastille Cornwallis

So hear ye hear ye, and you go on and Rise, Oh Silence of the Acadian Lambs, since it is all sinking into Kijpuktuk The Great harbour assimilation real quick; hence the call out and call to action. It is the civil obligation of Contemporary Artists to move the needle forward, inspiring readers to be empathetic shining agents of real and lasting change in Acadie's journey towards ending the ever-quickening assimilation via lack of representation in mainstream Haligonia-centric Bell Hony Media, like Theriault-calls out for in your face exclusion, since they are working on a template 1984 with no change.
In the formula, there are fresh talking heads of Hard Times in th Beep Suckin' Maritimes, don't you know?

Hence, there is need for a real creative renaissance with a benchmark template and playlist of AI and Blockchain platforms that can take well crafted `Meaning-written bullet point ideas like Theriault feeds in for visual illustrations for his KDP books, then take them and lay down ideas you can use to create fresh content reflective of the sign the times for real and in so doing keep creating; in the year of what many are calling the last Congrés Mondial Acadian 2024.

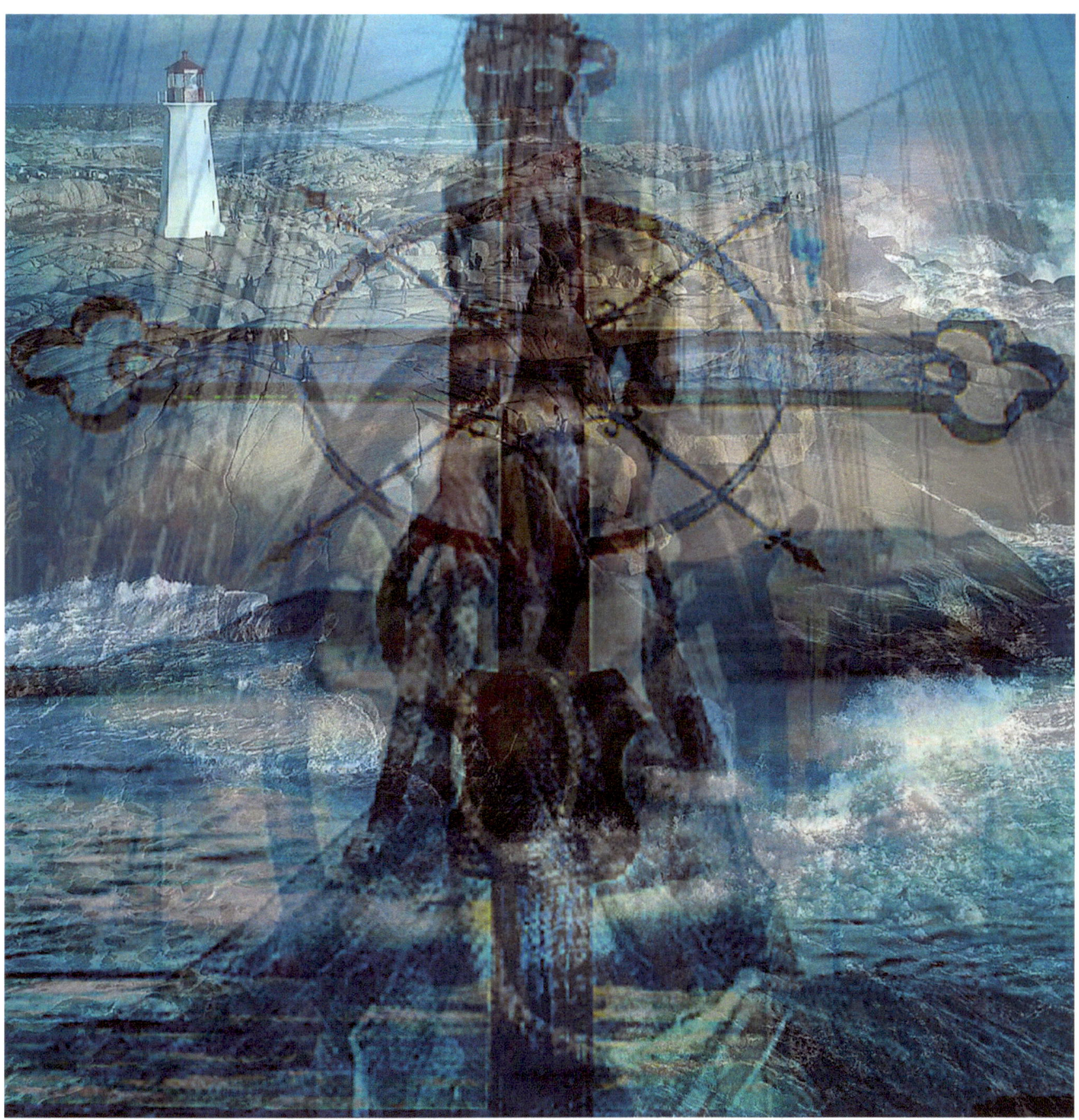

Chapter 16: Once you move forward you never look back.

The French Canadians in Quebec went through all of this in the Duplessie era, called La Grand Noirceur, which was draconian and dogmatic in 1937; we, as Acadians, are in that period now.
I don't wish to offend; I am just saying it since it needs saying.
To get somewhere, a culture has to start somewhere and have real empathetic people who know how to live it, and it isn't happening as long as we have The Silence of the Acadian Lambs doing nothing to unveil the Oligarchal Grip on <u>Creative & Innovation in the collapse of the Heritage Patrimonial Industry due to the Creative Bankruptcy</u> manifesto state it is in.
Contemporary Artists' civil obligation is to undo the mise en plie updo hairdo of ruling elitist types who answer to no one since they are not called upon to do so until you burn their Cultural Bordello to the ground with words.

French Acadian Culture will only move forward if it always looks back on its proud and noble Maritime Heritage. Even June Deveau gets no love or mention, just musicians and nothing but musicians making up Nos artistes de la Baie click and clan of politically connected snobs who answer to no one.

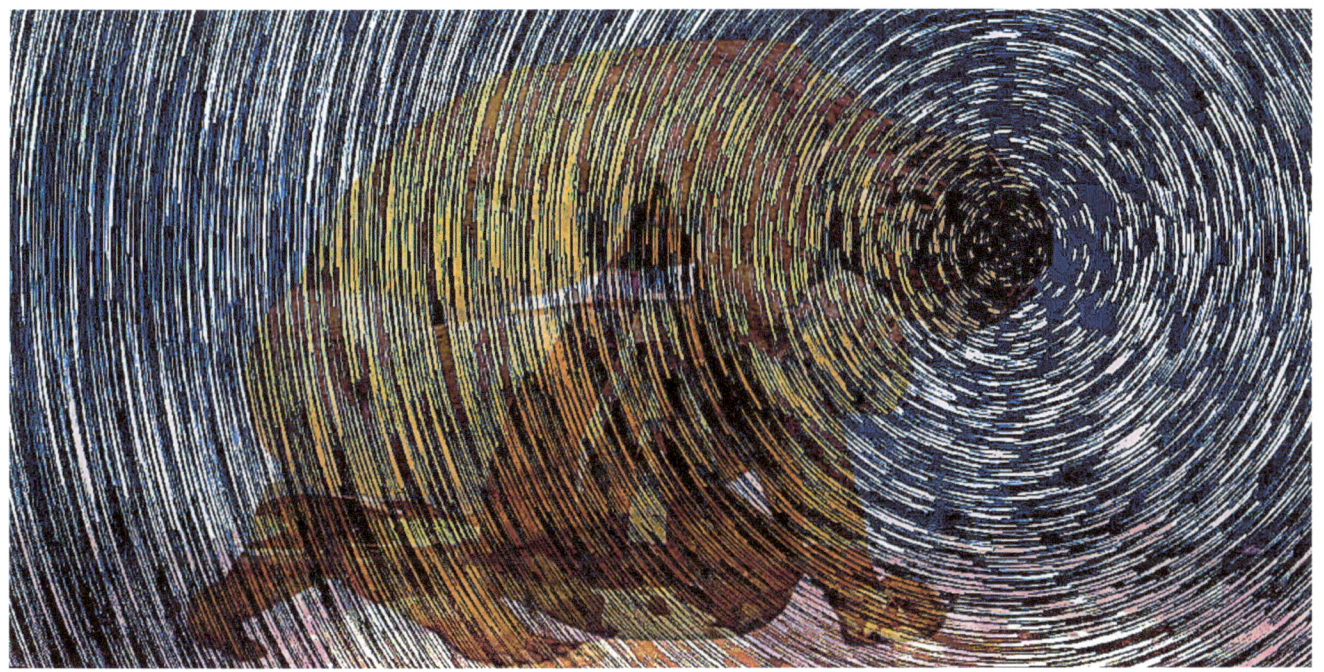

It is all part of the massive collapse of meaning itself that we see globally. It all moves us towards the <u>Great Reset of 2030</u>, a comin' around the bend. It is a feedback loop cycle called the Saeculum with the complete renewal of the human population. Creatives are aware of this, while Oligarchs are not; they think they can keep on running Zombie corporations that produce nothing. Like the Atlas Shrugged book, the ones with all the money and power had no morals or values, while the ones with morals and values had no money or power. Hence the need to call out since the only human rights you get these days are the ones you stand up and bitch to get, ask women, blacks and Indigenous people. They will tell you how the system works.

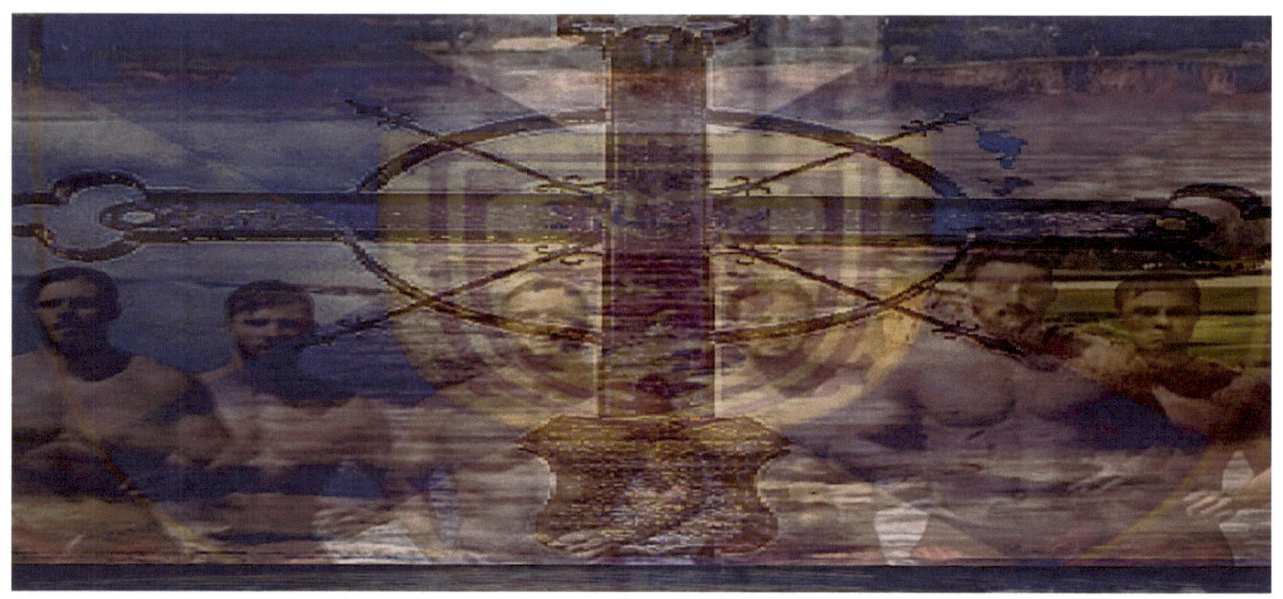

As you synchronize your breath with the rhythmic motion of the compass bow rotational cycle depicted in these exquisite motion graphics, distractions fade away, allowing you to enter a state of flow.

This immersive practice liberates you from the clutter of thoughts and distractions, enabling you to tap into your inner potential and pursue your life's purpose with clarity and focus. By aligning your breath with the visual cues provided by the <u>Mandala Mudra and Theriault's</u> motion graphics, you embark on a journey of self-discovery and optimization.